Simple
But Not
Easy

Simple But Not Easy

A Practical Guide to Taking the 12 Steps of Alcoholics Anonymous

---

Paul H. and Scott N.

Spiritual Progress Publishing Company

ISBN-13: 978-0-985559-60-1

LCCN: 2013917943

The first edition of *Alcoholics Anonymous* was published in 1939. It has since entered the public domain in the United States. The page and paragraph numbers from *Alcoholics Anonymous* referenced in *Simple But Not Easy* are taken from the fourth edition published in 2001. Citations to the Study Edition of *Alcoholics Anonymous*, published by The Anonymous Press, are also provided where the pagination differs.

For more information regarding this book, go to **www. SimpleButNotEasy.org**. There you can (1) communicate with the authors, (2) download Fourth Step worksheets, suggested prayers and other helpful materials, (3) learn where to buy additional copies of *Simple But Not Easy,* and (4) see a calendar of upcoming twelve-step seminars featuring the authors.

This book and its publication has not been authorized or endorsed by Alcoholics Anonymous World Services, Inc. ("AAWS"). The authors, this book, and **www.SimpleButNotEasy.org** are not affiliated with AAWS in any way. This book is not for sale outside the United States of America.

"WE, OF Alcoholics Anonymous, are more than one hundred men and women who have recovered from a seemingly hopeless state of mind and body. To show other alcoholics *precisely how we have recovered* is the main purpose of this book."

—Foreword to the first edition of

Alcoholics Anonymous (1939)

CONTENTS

ABOUT THIS BOOK

*T*he purpose of this book is simple: Extract the principles of the Big Book to help people understand the 12 Steps as explained therein, and then take those steps to achieve recovery from alcoholism. AA co-founder Bill Wilson described the program succinctly in recounting his own recovery:

> Simple, but not easy; a price had to be paid. It meant the destruction of self-centeredness. I must turn in all things to the Father of Light who presides over us all. BB 14:1

This guiding principle and the caution that we embrace "the simplicity of our program" expressed by AA co-founder Dr. Bob Smith are the inspiration for this book. Simple as the program may be, it requires deliberate action:

> Almost none of us liked the self-searching, the leveling of our pride, the confession of shortcomings which the process requires for its successful consummation. BB 25:1

Dr. Bob also addresses the level of effort required in his own story of recovery:

> [If] you really and truly want to quit drinking liquor for good and all, and sincerely feel that you must have some help, we know that we have an answer for

you. It never fails, if you go about it with one half the zeal you have been in the habit of showing when you were getting another drink. BB 181:2

This volume is not a replacement or substitute for the Big Book, the wonderful old textbook of recovery. In fact, it is intended to complement the Big Book. The authors hope it will serve as a guide for newcomers and sponsors and as a tool for Big Book study groups and seminars. You should read "The Doctor's Opinion" and chapters 1 through 7 in the Big Book before beginning.

This book, *Simple But Not Easy*, has one chapter devoted to each of the 12 Steps of Alcoholics Anonymous, as well as some important transitions between the steps. Each chapter incorporates text directly from the Big Book (BB), or careful paraphrasing, that relates to that step or twelve-step concept, followed by some notes from the authors. The passages are organized to describe "a design for living" (BB 28:2) that works for "anyone or everyone interested in a spiritual way of life" (BB 160:0).

Throughout this guide, references to the Big Book include the page number followed by the paragraph number where they can be found. A paragraph beginning on the previous page is identified with a zero ("0"). The page numbers and paragraphs refer to the fourth edition of *Alcoholics Anonymous*, published in 2001. The Study Edition of the Big Book published by Anonymous Press (AP)—which we highly recommend and use in our twelve-step seminars—has a few differing page citations in the front matter (those Roman-numbered pages preceding the main text), so we have also included citations to those pages.

In the Big Book, text of particular importance is printed in italics, and the quotes in this book retain that emphasis. Where the authors want to make additional emphasis in this volume, text from the Big Book is set in bold.

In the introduction to this book, the authors present some general observations and insights about the twelve-step program and the Fellowship of AA. In each subsequent chapter, there are Big Book passages followed by notes from the authors of this book. These notes were designed to aid in first understanding and then taking the steps, but are not offered as authoritative. Some readers may differ with these views. Although the authors believe their ideas are faithful to the Big Book in every way, they encourage thoughtful debate to the contrary.

INTRODUCTION TO THE 12-STEP SPIRITUAL
PROGRAM OF RECOVERY

A Bit of History About AA, the Big Book,
and Its Promise of Recovery

*A*lcoholics Anonymous was founded on June 10, 1935, the day AA co-founder Dr. Bob Smith took his last drink and commenced working a "program of spiritual action." He achieved his recovery from alcoholism with the assistance of co-founder Bill Wilson, who had recovered himself in December 1934 on the advice of a friend in the Oxford Group, a non-denominational Christian fellowship of the time.

The growth of AA was agonizingly slow in its early years. The first one hundred recovered men and women published a book in 1939 describing their collective experience of how a spiritual recovery from alcoholism could be achieved. That book, *Alcoholics Anonymous*, came to be known as the "Big Book" and through its fourth edition remains substantially unchanged. In every edition of the Big Book, Bill W's recovery story is chapter 1 and "Dr. Bob's Nightmare" is the first account in the "Personal Stories" section.

For over seventy years the Big Book of *Alcoholics Anonymous* has offered alcoholics a solution to their chronic, progressive, and fatal illness. This solution cannot be found in fighting or quitting or any other human effort.

Those willing to follow the 12 Steps as explained in this textbook of recovery will realize the benefits of this purely spiritual solution. When the work of the Big Book is complete, the "great promise" will be fulfilled:

> And we have ceased fighting anything or anyone— even alcohol. For by this time sanity will have returned. We will seldom be interested in liquor. If tempted, we recoil from it as from a hot flame. We react sanely and normally, and we will find that this has happened automatically. We will see that our new attitude toward liquor has been given us without any thought or effort on our part. It just comes! That is the miracle of it. We are not fighting it, neither are we avoiding temptation. We feel as though we had been placed in a position of neutrality—safe and protected. We have not even sworn off. Instead, the problem has been removed. It does not exist for us. We are neither cocky nor are we afraid. That is our experience. That is how we react so long as we keep in fit spiritual condition. BB 84:3

This small book offers newcomers, sponsors, and even long-time members of the AA Fellowship a new tool to identify and understand the basic principles of the Big Book. Once that understanding turns to action—taking the 12 Steps—a spiritual awakening and true recovery can be achieved by anyone.

THE TRUE NATURE OF THE STEPS

*T*he complete text of the 12 Steps are found only on pages 59 and 60 in the Big Book. Here they are:

1. We admitted we were powerless over alcohol—that our lives had become unmanageable.
2. Came to believe that a Power greater than ourselves could restore us to sanity.
3. Made a decision to turn our will and our lives over to the care of God *as we understood Him*.
4. Made a searching and fearless moral inventory of ourselves.
5. Admitted to God, to ourselves, and to another human being the exact nature of our wrongs.
6. Were entirely ready to have God remove all these defects of character.
7. Humbly asked Him to remove our shortcomings.
8. Made a list of all persons we had harmed, and became willing to make amends to them all.
9. Made direct amends to such people wherever possible, except when to do so would injure them or others.
10. Continued to take personal inventory and when we were wrong promptly admitted it.
11. Sought through prayer and meditation to improve our conscious contact with God *as we understood Him*, praying only for knowledge of His will for us and the power to carry that out.
12. Having had a spiritual awakening as the result of these steps, we tried to carry this message to alcoholics, and to practice these principles in all our affairs.

These are merely an outline or skeleton of the "spiritual program of action" (BB 85:1). This list of 12 Steps—as so many see hanging on the wall in AA meeting rooms—never hurt anyone. They may provide some relief to those suffering; however, no one ever achieved a spiritual awakening and resulting recovery from alcoholism by attempting to follow these cryptic suggestions alone.

The Big Book fleshes out the steps by first describing in precise detail how to take them and then revealing the results that we will experience in the process. These instructions make it clear that we must be expeditious and diligent in proceeding through the steps. Furthermore, we must take them in the designated sequence. They are action directions, not a list of rules (e.g., the Ten Commandments). For all these reasons, it is very important for newcomers to seek the help of a sponsor in taking these steps.

One way to think about the process of the 12 Steps is:

Step 1: The Problem

Step 2: The Solution

Step 3: The Decision to Move from the Problem to the Solution

Steps 4–9: The Action We Take to Implement the Decision

Steps 10–12: The Maintenance and Growth of Our Spiritual Recovery

It is the Program of Action, particularly Steps 4 through 9, that brings about a spiritual awakening and recovery. Merely discussing the steps in meetings or in coffee shops with other alcoholics will not achieve this result. We have to act!

Once we achieve recovery, the last three steps ensure the maintenance and growth of our spiritual experience and continued recovered life.

WE ARE RECOVERED, NOT "RECOVERING," ALCOHOLICS

Often in AA meetings we hear people refer to themselves as a "recovering alcoholic." The authors believe the term "recovered alcoholic" is more consistent with the message of the Big Book and its promise of recovery. In the first 164 pages of the Big Book, the term "recovered" is used seventeen times to describe the result of the steps. Most notably, the title page of the book (as a self-description) states: "The Story of How Many Thousands of Men and Women Have Recovered from Alcoholism" (BB iii).

On the other hand, the term "recovering" is used only once (BB 122:1; aside from a footnote in chapter 8, "To the Wives"), in reference to a wife's need to tolerate a husband who is still "convalescing" (BB 127:0). So while we are not "cured" of alcoholism (BB 85:1), we are recovered: "We have recovered and have been given the power to help others" (BB 132:2).

ABSTINENCE IS NOT RECOVERY

Many people abstain from alcohol for months, even years, by going to meetings, reciting the steps, and exchanging complaints about their lives with other abstinent people. For these people "not drinking" is their only goal. But abstinence is only the beginning of recovery (BB 19:1).

The authors will gladly send a thousand dollars to anyone who can find anywhere in the Big Book where it suggests to the alcoholic that he or she should "quit drinking." Saying that would destroy Step 1. We have no power over alcohol, so the Big Book does not frustrate its purpose by telling us to quit.

"Don't Drink and Go to Meetings"

We hear this refrain from well-intentioned people who are unfamiliar with the Big Book's program of recovery. The fallacy of this advice can be found in the first two sentences of "How It Works," the text recited at meetings thousands of times each day all around the world:

> Rarely have we seen a person fail who has thoroughly followed our path. Those who do not recover are people who cannot or will not completely give themselves to this simple program. BB 58:1

The promise of recovery is found in the program, not the organized Fellowship of AA. The risk of failure lies in refusing to follow the steps, not missing meetings. The Fellowship of AA, however helpful, is still human, and the Big Book makes it clear that "probably no human power could relieve our alcoholism." (BB 60:2). Our recovery rests upon a "spiritual program of action" (BB 85:1).

Meetings are rarely mentioned in the Big Book and generally concern happy social gatherings with other recovered people. The only exception is a reference to weekly meetings in the early years of AA that were "to be attended by anyone or everyone interested in a spiritual way of life," where the prime objective was to "provide a time and place where new people might bring their problems" (BB 159:3).

Two important points. First, anyone seeking a spiritual life was welcome in those meetings, much like the "open" meetings of today's AA. But even more than that, the Big Book recognized that everyone suffers from the spiritual malady, not just alcoholics. The thought was that anyone could benefit from the spiritual program of recovery. Second, the meeting was for newcomers and their problems, not the problems of recovered people. Dr. Dan Anderson, longtime president of the Hazelden Foundation and noted alcoholism scholar, often said in patient lectures: "The two purposes of the AA Fellowship are didactic [teaching and learning about the program of recovery] and inspirational [sharing our experience with the common solution to our alcohol problem]."

Chapter 11, "A Vision for You," is obviously addressed to those scattered people who had no Fellowship to rely upon and recovered solely by studying the content of the Big Book and following the steps (BB 151–164). So, once again, the message of the Big Book is focused on the Program of Action and the power of God, not the frequency of meetings.

FIGHTING WORDS

The first fruit of entering the world of the Spirit is the realization that we are no longer fighting anything or anyone, even alcohol. And this—the absence of fighting—is an indicator that sanity has returned. It sets the stage for removal of our obsession without thought or effort on our part—particularly quitting drinking.

We should be very cautious about accepting advice that encourages us to continue any fight, however well-meaning. Phrases like "Don't drink and _____" are always about a fighting tactic for alcohol. Step 1 teaches us the fallacy of this advice: "We admitted we were powerless over alcohol" (BB 59:2).

Powerlessness

We often hear at meetings that in addition to alcohol, we have no power over "people, places, or things." The truth is that we have no control over other people, situations, or outcomes, but we do have power in many areas.

However powerless over alcohol we are, we still have the power to take the steps that are the suggested "program of recovery" (BB 59:2).

> Simple, but not easy; a price had to be paid. It meant destruction of self-centeredness. BB 14:1.

That is how the Big Book describes the action to be taken on the path to recovery, and you have the power to pay the price.

And the Big Book tells us that we have the power to help others, once we have achieved our own recovery (BB 132:2).

So we are not powerless over everything. Don't use it as an excuse to do nothing. Remember the words of the "Serenity Prayer" and change the things you can:

> God grant me the serenity to accept the things I cannot change; courage to change the things I can; and wisdom to know the difference.

What Do You Need to Begin?

All that is necessary is the desire to stop drinking and the ability to exercise certain positive attitudes: willingness, honesty, and open-mindedness. The Big Book tells us this over and over.

> The only requirement for membership is an honest desire to stop drinking. BB xiv:0

Upon a foundation of complete willingness I might build what I saw in my friend. Would I have it? Of course I would! BB 12:4

Belief in the power of God, plus enough willingness, honesty and humility to establish and maintain the new order of things, were the essential requirements. BB 13:5

We have emphasized willingness as being indispensable. BB 76:1

To duplicate, with such backing, what we have accomplished is only a matter of willingness, patience and labor. BB 163:1

Willingness, honesty and open mindedness are the essentials of recovery. But these are indispensable. BB 568:3

How long do you want to wait to get well? Let's begin right now.

THE PROBLEM: NO POWER

"We admitted we were powerless over alcohol—that our lives had become unmanageable."

Learn about the step: BB xxv–xxxii (AP xxiii–xxx),
1–8, 18–24, 30–43
Take the step: BB 30:2

THE BODY PROBLEM: CRAVING FOR MORE AFTER THAT FIRST DRINK

"Lack of power, that was our dilemma." BB 45:1

"We believe, and so suggested a few years ago, that the action of alcohol on these chronic alcoholics is a manifestation of an allergy; that the phenomenon of craving is limited to this class and never occurs in the average temperate drinker." BB xxviii:1 (AP xxvi:1)

Alcoholics have an "allergy to alcohol" that causes a craving for more alcohol after it is ingested. BB xxvi:3, xxix:0, xxx:5 (AP xxiv:3, xxvii:0, xxviii:5)

Alcoholics are "not drinking to escape; they [are] drinking to overcome a craving beyond their mental control." BB xxx:0 (AP xxviii:0)

"All these, and many others, have one symptom in common: they cannot start drinking without developing the phenomenon of craving. This phenomenon, as we have suggested, may be the manifestation of an allergy that differentiates these people, and sets them apart as a distinct entity. It has never been, by any treatment with which we are familiar, permanently eradicated. The only relief we have to suggest is entire abstinence." BB xxx:5 (AP xxviii:5)

"The insanity of alcohol returns and we drink again. And with us, to drink is to die." BB 66:1

Ultimately, because the disease of alcoholism is progressive, for the alcoholic to drink is fatal. BB 15:0, 30:1, 24:4, 66:1, 154:4

THE MIND PROBLEM: SOBER OBSESSION THAT IT'S SAFE TO DRINK

"The idea that somehow, someday he will control and enjoy his drinking is the great obsession of every abnormal drinker. The persistence of this illusion is astonishing. Many pursue it into the gates of insanity or death." BB 30:1

"We alcoholics are men and women who have lost the ability to control our drinking. We know that no real alcoholic *ever* recovers control. All of us felt at times that we were regaining control, but such intervals—usually brief—were inevitably followed by still less control, which led in time to pitiful and incomprehensible demoralization. We are convinced to a man that alcoholics of our type are in the grip of a progressive illness. Over any considerable period we get worse, never better." BB 30:3

"*The fact is that most alcoholics, for reasons yet obscure, have lost the power of choice in drink.*" BB 24:1

"How then shall we help our readers determine, to their own satisfaction, whether they are one of us? The experiment of quitting for a period of time will be helpful, but we think we can render an even greater service to alcoholic sufferers and perhaps to the medical fraternity. So we shall describe some of the mental states that precede a relapse into drinking, for obviously this is the crux of the problem." BB 34:3–35:0

"This is the baffling feature of alcoholism as we know it— this utter inability to leave it alone, no matter how great the necessity or the wish." BB 34:2

"*We are without defense against the first drink.*" BB 24:1

"Once more: The alcoholic at certain times has no effective mental defense against the first drink." BB 43:3

PERSONAL HOPELESSNESS

"We OF Alcoholics Anonymous, are more than one hundred men and women who have recovered from a seemingly **hopeless** state of mind and body." BB xiii

"We, of Alcoholics Anonymous, know thousands of men and women who were once just as **hopeless** as Bill. Nearly all have recovered. They have solved the drink problem." BB 17:1

"[W]e have recovered from a **hopeless** condition of mind and body." BB 20:1

"Almost none of us liked the self-searching, the leveling of our pride, the confession of shortcomings which the process requires for its successful consummation. But we saw that it really worked in others, and we had come to believe in the **hopelessness** and futility of life as we had been living it." BB 25:1

"In the doctor's judgment he was utterly **hopeless**; he could never regain his position in society and he would have to place himself under lock and key or hire a bodyguard if he expected to live long." BB 26:3

"What you say about the general hopelessness of the average alcoholic's plight is, in my opinion, correct. As to two of you men, whose stories I have heard, there is no doubt in

my mind that you were 100% **hopeless**, apart from divine help."
BB 43:2

UNMANAGEABILITY

"[W]e were alcoholic and could not manage our own lives." BB 60:2

"They are restless, irritable and discontented, unless they can again experience the sense of ease and comfort which comes at once by taking a few drinks—drinks which they see others taking with impunity." BB xxviii:4 (AP xxvi:4)

"We were having trouble with personal relationships, we couldn't control our emotional natures, we were a prey to misery and depression, we couldn't make a living, we had a feeling of uselessness, we were full of fear, we were unhappy, we couldn't seem to be of real help to other people—was not a basic solution of these bedevilments more important than whether we should see newsreels of lunar flight? Of course it was." BB 52: 2

An alcoholic is "a victim of the delusion that he can wrest satisfaction and happiness out of this world if he only manages well." BB 61:1

Alcoholics lead lives typified by: a need to control, self-pity, self-delusion, self-seeking, self-will run riot, and God playing. BB 60–62

HOW DO YOU TAKE STEP 1?

"We learned that we had to fully concede to our innermost selves that we were alcoholics. This is the first step in recovery." BB 30:2

"If we are planning to stop drinking, there must be no reservation of any kind, nor any lurking notion that someday we will be immune to alcohol." BB 33:1

NOTES ON STEP 1

No Power Over Alcohol

The Big Book teaches us that all alcoholics face inevitable consequences. First, we have a body problem—the craving for more alcohol once we take the first drink. Second, we have a mind problem—at certain times we are obsessed with the false notion that we can control and enjoy our drinking, like a "normal" person. Our powerlessness over alcohol is demonstrated by a simple equation.

Consequence of the Body Problem = Can't Drink
Consequence of the Mental Problem = Can't Quit
Can't Drink + Can't Quit = NO POWER

By recognizing this dilemma, we understand and accept our powerlessness over alcohol and give direction to our personal hopelessness, thus beginning the process of recovery.

Finding Your Real Bottom

Many newcomers to AA wonder if they have reached their "bottom," having heard that it is a fundamental part of Step 1. That "bottom" is often described in terms of the horrible events and outcomes experienced by the alcoholic. Certainly, being honest about our alcoholic life helps demonstrate our powerlessness over alcohol, but terrible consequences alone do not bring us to our "bottom" in AA—the place where we can begin to recover.

Your "real bottom" is not an external event. It is the moment you admit to yourself that:

1. you lack any power over alcohol,
2. your life has become hopeless as a consequence of that powerlessness, and

3. neither you nor any other human can solve the problem (BB 60:3).

Our lack of power over alcohol continues throughout our lives—recovered or not. The physical consequence of taking the first drink and the obsession that prevents us from quitting are ongoing realities for all of us. Recognizing that problem is your "real bottom."

Taking Step 1 is evidence of a desire to stop drinking and an awareness of the problem we face. It gives reality, understanding, and direction to our hopeless situation, even if we do not yet recognize the solution. Our utter hopelessness provides us with a place to begin.

An Unmanageable Life

You probably know if your life has "become unmanageable," if you are "restless, irritable, and discontented" when you are not drinking (BB xxviii:4; AP xxvi:4). But if you are unsure, consider the "Bedevilments" facing the alcoholic as described in the Big Book:

> We were having trouble with personal relationships, we couldn't control our emotional natures, we were a prey to misery and depression, we couldn't make a living, we had a feeling of uselessness, we were full of fear, we were unhappy, we couldn't seem to be of real help to other people . . . BB 52:2

Next, most AAs are familiar with the spiritual "promises" that the Big Book offers "before we are halfway through" the 9th Step (BB 83:4). The life of an unrecovered alcoholic—abstinent or not—can be described in terms of those "9th Step Promises" **in reverse**:

Know a lack of freedom and happiness. Regret the past and wish to shut the door on it. Fail to comprehend serenity and to know peace. Lack understanding of how your experience can benefit others. Feel uselessness and self-pity. Be interested only in selfish things and have little or no interest in your fellows. Self-seeking grows with each passing day. Fear of people and economic insecurity increases, too. Remain clueless on how to handle baffling situations. Do everything yourself—without success.

Can you find yourself in these descriptions? This is the unmanageable life that Step 1 acknowledges.

Step 1 Perfection

We must get and hang on to Step 1, **perfectly**. It is reality. It is the problem.

Step 1 is not a "spiritual principle" like the following eleven steps that seek to solve the problem. Those "spiritual principles" defy perfection, but Step 1 does not (BB 60:2).

Step 2

THE SOLUTION: POWER GREATER THAN SELF

"Came to believe that a Power greater than ourselves could restore us to sanity."

Learn about the step: BB 9–16, 17, 25–29
Take the step: BB 47:2

WHERE IS THE POWER GREATER THAN SELF?

The alcoholic is "suffering from an illness which only a spiritual experience will conquer." BB 44:1

"Lack of power, that was our dilemma. We had to find a power by which we could live, and it had to be a *Power greater than ourselves*. Obviously. But **where** and **how** were we to find this Power?" BB 45:1

"[F]or deep down in every man, woman, and child, is the fundamental idea of God." BB 55:2

"Much to our relief, we discovered we did not need to consider another's conception of God. Our own conception, however inadequate, was sufficient to make the approach and to effect a contact with Him." BB 46:2

HOW DO WE FIND THE POWER GREATER THAN SELF?

"Well, that's exactly what this book is about. Its main object is to enable you to find a Power greater than yourself which will solve your problem. That means we have written a book which we believe to be spiritual as well as moral. And it means, of course, that we are going to talk about God." BB 45:2

"To show other alcoholics PRECISELY HOW WE HAVE RECOVERED is the main purpose of this book." BB xiii:1

"Here are the steps we took, which are suggested as a program of recovery . . ." BB 59:2

WHAT IS THE RELATIONSHIP BETWEEN GOD AND RECOVERY?

"[W]e had to fearlessly face the proposition that either God is everything or else He is nothing. God either is, or He isn't. What was our choice to be?" BB 53:2

"Our ideas did not work. But the God idea did." BB 52:3

"The central fact of our lives today is the absolute certainty that our Creator has entered into our hearts and lives in a way which is indeed miraculous. **He has commenced to accomplish those things for us which we could never do by ourselves.**" BB 25:2

"Once more: The alcoholic at certain times has no effective mental defense against the first drink. Except in a few rare cases, neither he nor any other human being can provide such a defense. His defense must come from a Higher Power." BB 43:3

"Without help it is too much for us. But there is One who has all power—that One is God. May you find Him now!" BB 59:0

THE CHOICE

"We were in a position where life was becoming impossible, and if we had passed into the region from which there is no return through human aid, we had but two alternatives: One was to go on to the bitter end, blotting out the consciousness of our intolerable situation as best we could; and the other, to accept spiritual help." BB 25:3

"To be doomed to an alcoholic death or to live on a spiritual basis are not always easy alternatives to face." BB 44:2

How Do You Take Step 2?

"We needed to ask ourselves but one short question. 'Do I now believe, or am I even willing to believe, that there is a Power greater than myself?' As soon as a man can say that he does believe, or is willing to believe, we emphatically assure him that he is on his way. It has been repeatedly proven among us that upon this simple cornerstone a wonderfully effective spiritual structure can be built." BB 47:2

Notes on Step 2

The Simplicity of Step 2

Consider the simplicity of Step 2. It does not suggest that we find or embrace any particular God, religion, or doctrine. This entirely spiritual structure of recovery rests only on a belief or willingness to believe that **we are not the highest power in the universe—we are not God**.

Bill W, AA's co-founder, learned this simple truth when his friend Ebby Thatcher asked him: "*Why don't you choose your own conception of God?*" (BB 12:2).

Bill W explained:

That statement hit me hard. It melted the icy intellectual mountain in whose shadow I had lived and shivered many years. I stood in the sunlight at last.

It was only a matter of being willing to believe in a Power greater than myself. Nothing more was required of me to make my beginning. I saw that growth could start from that point. Upon a foundation of complete willingness I might build what I saw in my friend. Would I have it? Of course I would!

Thus was I convinced that God is concerned with us humans when we want Him enough. At long last I saw, I felt, I believed. Scales of pride and prejudice fell from my eyes. A new world came into view. BB 12:2–12:5

Although it may not be your final destination, your own conception of God is a necessary place to start. It's where you are now.

Coming to Believe Through the Experience of Others

Someone who has had a spiritual awakening or experience and has recovered as the result of taking the 12 Steps should guide newcomers to the program. The experiences of others in recovery can be the basis for the belief necessary to take Step 2. Just as Bill W responded to Ebby's recovery and suggestion, so too can a "sponsee" (one who is sponsored) rely upon a sponsor's experience. The Big Book tells us:

When, therefore, we were approached by those in whom the problem had been solved, there was nothing left for us but to pick up the simple kit of spiritual tools laid at our feet. BB 25:1

Throughout our lives we rely upon the recommendations and suggestions of those people we trust, respect, and admire. If we "believe" what they tell us, we may act on their suggestion. When the outcome is favorable, we develop personal "faith" in the recommendation. In the same way, we can embark on the path to recovery based upon our "belief" in the suggestions of a sponsor or the Big Book itself—the collected wisdom of the first one hundred recovered alcoholics in AA. Our own recovery experience then forms the basis for our "faith" in the program and we can pass it along to those in need of a solution.

What Is a Higher Power and What Is Not?

The word "God" is used 131 times in the primary text of the Big Book, while the term "higher power" is used only twice, and in both cases the term clearly refers to an all-powerful deity:

> Once more: The alcoholic at certain times has no effective mental defense against the first drink. Except in a few rare cases, neither he nor any other human being can provide such a defense. His defense must come from a **Higher Power**. BB 43:3

> Both you and the new man must walk day by day in the path of spiritual progress. If you persist, remarkable things will happen. When we look back, we realize that the things which came to us when we put ourselves in God's hands were better than anything we could have planned. Follow the dictates of a **Higher Power** and you will presently live in a

new and wonderful world, no matter what your present circumstances! BB 100:1

So, ultimately your sponsor, your AA group, your treatment center, your husband/wife, or any other human force cannot be the Higher Power that brings about your recovery.

Remember that we deal with alcohol—cunning, baffling, powerful! Without help it is too much for us. But there is One who has all power—that One is God. BB 58:4

Step 3

DECIDING TO MOVE FROM THE PROBLEM TO THE SOLUTION

"Made a decision to turn our will and our lives over to the care of God as we understood Him."

Learn about the step: BB 60-63
Take the step: BB 63:2

Big Book ABCs

In order to take Step 3, you must complete Steps 1 and 2. The essence of those steps is in "the Big Book's ABCs":

"Our description of the alcoholic, the chapter to the agnostic, and our personal adventures before and after make clear three pertinent ideas:

a) That we were alcoholic and could not manage our own lives.

b) That probably no human power could have relieved our alcoholism.

c) That God could and would if He were sought." BB 60:2

Spiritual Sickness and Recovery

"The first requirement is that we be convinced that any life run on self-will can hardly be a success. On that basis we are almost always in collision with something or somebody, even though our motives are good. **Most people try to live by self-propulsion. Each person is like an actor who wants to run**

the whole show; is forever trying to arrange the lights, the ballet, the scenery and the rest of the players in his own way. If his arrangements would only stay put, if only people would do as he wished, the show would be great. Everybody, including himself, would be pleased. Life would be wonderful. In trying to make these arrangements our actor may sometimes be quite virtuous. He may be kind, considerate, patient, generous; even modest and self-sacrificing. On the other hand, he may be mean, egotistical, selfish and dishonest. But, as with most humans, he is more likely to have varied traits." BB 60:4–61:0

"What usually happens? The show doesn't come off very well. He begins to think life doesn't treat him right. He decides to exert himself more. He becomes, on the next occasion, still more demanding or gracious, as the case may be. Still the play does not suit him. Admitting he may be somewhat at fault, he is sure that other people are more to blame. He becomes angry, indignant, self-pitying. What is his basic trouble? Is he not really a self-seeker even when trying to be kind? Is he not a victim of the delusion that he can wrest satisfaction and happiness out of this world if he only manages well? Is it not evident to all the rest of the players that these are the things he wants? And do not his actions make each of them wish to retaliate, snatching all they can get out of the show? Is he not, even in his best moments, a producer of confusion rather than harmony?" BB 61:1

"Selfishness—self-centeredness! That, we think, is the root of our troubles. Driven by a hundred forms of fear, self-delusion, self-seeking, and self-pity, we step on the toes of our fellows and they retaliate. Sometimes they hurt us, seemingly without provocation, but we invariably find that at some time in the past we have made decisions based on self which later placed us in a position to be hurt." BB 62:1

"So our troubles, we think, are basically of our own making. They arise out of ourselves, and the alcoholic is an extreme example of self-will run riot, though he usually doesn't think so. Above everything, we alcoholics must be rid of this selfishness. We must, or it kills us! God makes that possible. And there often seems no way of entirely getting rid of self without His aid." BB 62:2

"This is the how and why of it. First of all, we had to quit playing God. It didn't work." BB 62:3

"When the spiritual malady is overcome, we straighten out mentally and physically." BB 64:3

How Do We Take Step 3?
We take Step 3 **with another person** by praying the prayer in the Big Book:

"We were now at Step Three. Many of us said to our Maker, *as we understood Him*: 'God, I offer myself to Thee—to build with me and to do with me as Thou wilt. Relieve me of the bondage of self, that I may better do Thy will. Take away my difficulties, that victory over them may bear witness to those I would help of Thy Power, Thy Love, and Thy Way of life. May I do Thy will always!' We thought well before taking this step making sure we were ready; that we could at last abandon ourselves utterly to Him." BB 63:2

NOTES ON STEP 3

The Spiritual Malady

Our fundamental spiritual problem is that we want to play God (BB 62:3). The Big Book describes God-playing as being "self-centered" or "egocentric" (BB 61:2). Today we would call it the need to control.

Any true God has universal knowledge, judges perfectly, and controls everything (i.e., is always right). We don't have those qualities. That is why the Big Book tells us to quit playing God: "It didn't work" (BB 62:3).

Can't Change Without God's Help

We cannot change without God's help, and the 12 Steps are the path to that help. When God overcomes our spiritual malady, our physical and mental problems are removed (BB 64:3)—"It does not exist for us" (BB 85:0).

The **physical** and **mental** problems of alcoholics—"can't drink and can't quit"—separate us from other people (BB 30:1). However, our spiritual malady—"powerless to change" without God's help—is one that we share with all of humanity (BB 62:2). The self-centered, egocentric actor "who wants to run the whole show" (BB 61–62) is the essence of what today we call the person who always has a "need to control."

When describing this spiritual problem, the Big Book makes it plain that it affects everyone, not just alcoholics: "Most people try to live by self-propulsion" (BB 60:4). The consequence of this "selfishness—self-centeredness" (BB 62:1), "self-will run riot" (BB 62:2), and "playing God" (BB 62:3) may be more severe for alcoholics than for others—"it kills us" (BB 62:2). But the spiritual sickness is the same.

Decision to Seek a Spiritual Solution

Step 3 is a decision to embark on a six-step program of action (Steps 4 through 9) that will allow us to accept God's power to change our personalities in such a way as to bring about recovery from alcoholism (BB 567:1; AP 569:1). We then continue to grow spiritually by practicing Steps 10, 11, and 12 throughout the rest of our lives.

This "design for living" has nothing to do with drinking—alcohol is but a symptom. We have a problem of the body and mind that yields to a spiritual solution. As the senior author of this volume is often heard to say: "Talking about the spiritual part of the program is like talking about the wet part of the ocean!"

Our spiritual problem—and our alcoholism—is solved with God's power. But that relief only comes if we actually implement the third-step decision and take the remaining steps.

Step 4

DISCOVERING WHAT BLOCKS US FROM GOD'S POWER

"Made a searching and fearless moral inventory of ourselves."

Learn about the step: BB 64–71
Take the step: BB 64:2

What Is an "Inventory"?

"Though our decision [in Step 3] was a vital and crucial step, it could have little permanent effect unless at once followed by a strenuous effort to face, and to be rid of, the things in ourselves which had been blocking us. Our liquor was but a symptom. So we had to get down to causes and conditions." BB 64:0

"[W]e started upon a personal inventory. *This was Step Four.* A business which takes no regular inventory usually goes broke. Taking a commercial inventory is a fact-finding and a fact-facing process. It is an effort to discover the truth about the stock-in-trade." BB 64:1

"We did exactly the same thing with our lives. We took stock honestly. First, we searched out the flaws in our make-up which caused our failure [to exert power over alcohol]." BB 64:2; BB 45:1

WHEN DO WE TAKE AN INVENTORY?

"**Next** we launched out on a course of vigorous action, the first step of which is a personal housecleaning [Steps 4–7], which many of us had never attempted. Though our decision was a vital and crucial step [Step 3], it could have little permanent effect unless **at once** followed by a strenuous effort to face [Steps 4 and 5], and to be rid of [Steps 6 and 7], the things in ourselves which had been blocking us. Our liquor was but a symptom. So we had to get down to causes and conditions." BB 63:4

WHY DO WE TAKE AN INVENTORY?

"Being convinced that self, manifested in various ways, was what had defeated us, we considered its common manifestations." BB 64:2

"We have been trying to get a new attitude, a new relationship with our Creator, and to discover the obstacles in our path." BB 72:1

RESENTMENTS—THE NUMBER ONE OFFENDER

"Resentment is the 'number one' offender. It destroys more alcoholics than anything else. From it stem all forms of spiritual disease, for we have been not only mentally and physically ill, we have been spiritually sick. When the spiritual malady is overcome, we straighten out mentally and physically. In dealing with resentments, we set them on paper. We listed people, institutions or principles with whom we were angry. We asked ourselves why we were angry. In most cases it was found that our self-esteem, our pocketbooks, our ambitions, our personal relationships (including sex) were hurt or threatened. So we were sore. We were 'burned up.'" BB 64:3

"On our grudge list we set opposite each name our injuries. Was it our self-esteem, our security, our ambitions, our personal, or sex relations, which had been interfered with?" BB 65:1

"We turned back to the list, for it held the key to the future. We were prepared to look at it from an entirely different angle. We began to see that the world and its people really dominated us. In that state, the wrong-doing of others, fancied or real, had power to actually kill. How could we escape? We saw that these resentments must be mastered, but how? We could not wish them away any more than alcohol." BB 66:3

"This was our course. We realized that the people who wronged us were perhaps spiritually sick. Though we did not like their symptoms and the way these disturbed us, they, like ourselves, were sick too. We asked God to help us show them the same tolerance, pity, and patience that we would cheerfully grant a sick friend. When a person offended we said to ourselves, 'This is a sick man. How can I be helpful to him? God save me from being angry. Thy will be done.'" BB 66:4

"Referring to our list again. Putting out of our minds the wrongs others had done, we resolutely looked for our own mistakes. Where had we been selfish, dishonest, self-seeking and frightened? Though a situation had not been entirely our fault, we tried to disregard the other person involved entirely. Where were we to blame? The inventory was ours, not the other man's. When we saw our faults we listed them. We placed them before us in black and white. We admitted our wrongs honestly and were willing to set these matters straight." BB 67:2

Fear—Failure of Self-Reliance

"We reviewed our fears thoroughly. We put them on paper. . . . We asked ourselves why we had them. Wasn't it because self-reliance failed us? Self-reliance was good as far as it went, but it didn't go far enough." BB 68:1

"Perhaps there is a better way—we think so. For we are now on a different basis; the basis of trusting and relying upon God. We trust infinite God rather than our finite selves. We are in the world to play the role He assigns. Just to the extent that we do as we think He would have us, and humbly rely on Him, does He enable us to match calamity with serenity." BB 68:2

"We ask Him to remove our fear and direct our attention to what He would have us be. At once, we commence to outgrow fear." BB 68:3

Harms to Others—Selfish Relationships

"We have listed the people we have hurt by our conduct, and are willing to straighten out the past if we can." BB 70:3

"We reviewed our own conduct over the years past. Where had we been selfish, dishonest, or inconsiderate? Whom had we hurt? Did we unjustifiably arouse jealousy, suspicion or bitterness? Where were we at fault, what should we have done instead? We got this all down on paper and looked at it." BB 69:1

"In this way we tried to shape a sane and sound ideal for our future sex life. We subjected each relation to this test—was it selfish or not? We asked God to mold our ideals and help us to live up to them. We remembered always that our sex powers were God-given and therefore good, neither to be used lightly or selfishly nor to be despised and loathed." BB 69:2

"We earnestly pray for the right ideal, for guidance in each questionable situation, for sanity, and for the strength to do the right thing." BB 70:2

WHAT IS THE RESULT OF A THOROUGH 4TH STEP?

"In this book you read again and again that faith did for us what we could not do for ourselves. We hope you are convinced now that God can remove whatever self-will has blocked you off from Him. If you have already made a decision, and an inventory of your grosser handicaps, you have made a good beginning. That being so you have swallowed and digested some big chunks of truth about yourself." BB 70:4

NOTES ON STEP 4
Finding What Blocks Us from God

Socrates said, "The unexamined life is not worth living." Our 4th Step inventory is such an examination, and if done following the Big Book instructions it provides us with the information we need to complete the next five action steps. In the 4th Step we identify the personality defects that separate us from God's healing power. Its "searching and fearless moral inventory" is designed to do just that (BB 59:2).

There is a lot of fear and confusion surrounding this step, mostly created by those who have never completed a 4th Step inventory. The worksheets that are in the appendix to this book are designed to make the process as easy and simple as possible. Everything in these worksheets is based upon instructions in the Big Book.

Many people get loaded or act out in some way when they reach this step. Why? They will tell you that the pain of dredging up memories long buried was too much to endure, or any one of a thousand excuses. The plain and simple fact is just this: the pain does not come in writing this inventory; it comes in resisting the writing. Or even just starting the writing.

Alcoholics, time after time, would rather get drunk again than face some inner truths. The freedom from self is impossible when we hold onto the "old ideas" we have harbored all our lives (BB 58:3). The way of strength, paradoxically, is in becoming vulnerable.

It is time to find a new manner of thinking and acting, just as Dr. Bob did:

> "I then began asking a lot of questions of both my brother and Dr. Bob about how this thing worked, and I supposed I was becoming glassy-eyed all the while, for eventually I said to Bob, 'You're all dried up. You're never going to want another drink are you?'; and this answer of his is very important to those of us who are victims of alcoholism. He said, 'So long as I'm thinking as I'm thinking now, and so long as I'm doing the things I'm doing now, I don't believe I'll ever take another drink.'" *Alcoholics Anonymous*: Big Book, ("He Had to be Shown," third edition, Alcoholics Anonymous World Services, Inc., 1976, p. 206.)

Using Prayer to Resolve Our Resentments, Fears, and Wrongs

An essential part of doing your 4th Step inventory is utilizing the prayer suggestions for resentments, fears, and wrongs to others (BB 67:0; 68:3; 69:2, 3; 70:2). When we move into the 5th Step, those problems should have been prayerfully resolved or be well on the way to resolution. And in the 5th Step we will see "the exact nature of wrongs that brought about the resentments, fears and wrongs" in the first place—so we can ask God to remove those character defects and avoid recurrence.

Specific Guidance on Step 4

To be able to do Step 4, the previous Steps 1, 2, and 3 must have been completed (BB 63:4). So before starting, check with your sponsor to make sure you are ready.

Use the worksheets in the appendix of this book to guide you through the inventory process. They are designed to follow the specific instructions in the Big Book (BB 64–71).

Be honest! The only person to truly benefit from this process is you. Do not cheat yourself out of this incredible experience (BB 73:1).

This in an inventory of our "grosser handicaps," not the autobiography of Benjamin Franklin. Be thorough yet to the point (and not needlessly repetitious) (BB 71:0).

The inventory must be written (BB 64:3, 68:1, 69:1).

It should not take you more than a few days to complete your inventory.

Use the prayers. This is not a self-help program. We need to and humbly ask for God's help throughout the steps. Prayer helps us focus on our shortcomings and achieve a more truthful inventory (BB 67–70).

It may be helpful to think about your resentments, fears, and harms in terms of groups (i.e., family, school, relationships, work, etc.) so you can be complete.

Do not fill in your "grudge list" horizontally. Do it in columns (i.e., all names first, all causes second, etc.) (BB 64:3; 65:1).

The Big Book does not suggest listing assets against 4th Step resentments, fears, and wrongs. We will be basking in the glory of recovery in just a few days if we are diligent in our work. That is the greatest asset of all.

The Eight Parts of "Self"

In order to better understand the nature of our resentments, fears, and harms to others, we need to consider what aspects of ourselves are injured, affected, or threatened. Here are some suggested definitions for the aspects of self found in the Big Book and used in the inventory process (BB 65:1-2).

Self-Esteem	How we think of ourselves.
Emotional Security	Our general sense of personal well-being.
Financial Security	Our basic desire for money, property, possessions, etc.
Physical Security	Our need for safety and survival.
Personal Relations	Our relations with other people.
Sex Relations	Our basic drive for sexual intimacy and gratification, both acceptable and hidden.
Ambitions	Our goals, plans, and designs for the future.
Pride	How we think others view us.

These aspects of self are a necessary and proper part of human nature, but in excess they can cause spiritual damage and resulting character defects. So as we consider our resentments, fears, and wrongs, we also need to evaluate whether the aspects of self are appropriate or distorted.

The "Grudge List" is Not an Inventory

Some people mistake the "grudge list" or resentments list for their inventory. Your grudge list details the acts or threats from others that triggered your feelings of resentment. By looking for the character defects that bring about these feelings, we can identify those shortcomings that we need to have God remove in the 7th Step. That list of character defects or shortcomings is the "inventory." We are just as powerless over our resentments as we are over alcohol. So self-help—our own willpower—will not work. We need God's power to overcome resentments.

Step 5

SHARING AND UNDERSTANDING WHAT BLOCKS US FROM GOD'S POWER

"Admitted to God, to ourselves, and to another human being the exact nature of our wrongs."

Learn about the step: BB 72–75
Take the step: BB 75:1–2

WHAT ARE WE DOING?

"Having made our personal inventory, what shall we do about it? We have been trying to get a new attitude, a new relationship with our Creator, and to discover the obstacles in our path. We have admitted certain defects; we have ascertained in a rough way what the trouble is; we have put our finger on the weak items in our personal inventory. Now these are about to be cast out. This requires action on our part, which, when completed, will mean that we have admitted to God, to ourselves, and to another human being, the exact nature of our defects." BB 72:1

WITH WHOM?

"[W]e are very anxious that we talk to the right person. It is important that he be able to keep a confidence; that he fully understand and approve what we are driving at; that he will not try to change our plan." BB 74:2

"We explain to our partner what we are about to do and why we have to do it. He should realize that we are engaged upon a life-and-death errand." BB 75:1

WHEN?

"[W]e hold ourselves in complete readiness to go through with it at the first opportunity." BB 74:2

"When we decide who is to hear our story, we waste no time." BB 75:1

WHY?

"The best reason first: If we skip this vital step, we may not overcome drinking. Time after time newcomers have tried to keep to themselves certain facts about their lives. Trying to avoid this humbling experience, they have turned to easier methods. Almost invariably they got drunk. Having persevered with the rest of the program, they wondered why they fell. We think the reason is that they never completed their housecleaning. They took inventory all right, but hung on to some of the worst items in stock. They only *thought* they had lost their egoism and fear; they only *thought* they had humbled themselves. But they had not learned enough of humility, fearlessness and honesty, in the sense we find it necessary, until they told someone else *all* their life story." BB 72:2

SO DROP THE ACT!

"More than most people, the alcoholic leads a double life. He is very much the actor. To the outer world he presents his stage character. This is the one he likes his fellows to see. He wants to enjoy a certain reputation, but knows in his heart he doesn't deserve it." BB 73:1

How Do We Take Step 5?

"We pocket our pride and go to it, illuminating every twist of character, every dark cranny of the past. Once we have taken this step, withholding nothing, we are delighted." BB 75:2

What Is the Result of Step 5?

"We can look the world in the eye. We can be alone at perfect peace and ease. Our fears fall from us. We begin to feel the nearness of our Creator. We may have had certain spiritual beliefs, but now we begin to have a spiritual experience. The feeling that the drink problem has disappeared will often come strongly. We feel we are on the Broad Highway, walking hand in hand with the Spirit of the Universe." BB 75:2

Notes on Step 5

Choosing the Person to Hear Your 5th Step

The Big Book first suggests that we seek out a clergy member to hear our 5th Step (BB 74:0). This is good advice, if they are experienced with the 12 Steps. It is also advisable if matters of a criminal nature might be discussed, given the legal privilege afforded the clergy.

The Big Book goes on to suggest a "doctor or psychologist" as an alternative to a clergy person (BB 74:1). While this may have been an option in 1939—when the Big Book was published—it is not practical today. Imagine calling your local clinic to schedule a "5th Step."

Finally, the Big Book suggests a family member as a possible 5th Step participant (BB 74:1). Experience has shown this to be a truly dangerous course of action for obvious reasons.

At the time the Big Book was written, there were very few people who understood the 12 Steps or how to hear a 5th Step.

Perhaps that is the reason for some of the suggestions outlined in the Big Book. Today there are many qualified people who are anxious to be helpful in this way.

The authors strongly suggest that a sponsor or someone well-schooled in the 12 Steps be called upon to hear your 5th Step. As such, this individual will understand what you are doing, guide you through the process, and treat what you reveal as confidential.

How a 5th Step Might Begin

One of the authors of this book has heard hundreds of 5th Steps. He has never observed anything but delight, relief, or enthusiasm in a person completing the step. At the beginning of each 5th Step meeting, he says something like this:

> This is an opportunity for you to drop your "stage character" or any façade for an hour or two. See how it feels to be completely yourself. Nothing you say or do will ever be revealed to anyone else.

> This is your chance to talk about anything that you have never shared with another person and have been living with alone. You will experience a remarkable relief that comes in the sharing and the realization that you are not alone anymore.

> You will benefit enormously from this process, if you are truthful and complete. If not, you are the only person that will be harmed. So you have nothing to lose by utter frankness.

> Perhaps you should begin with the most difficult matter.

The Exact Nature of Our Wrongs

In the 5th Step we admit "the exact nature of our wrongs." Many reading this language believe the "wrongs" to be the actions or events we describe to God and the other person. In fact, the "wrongs" are the character defects that block us from God. A seasoned 5th Step participant will listen to your story while trying to find the shortcomings that thread their way through that story and your life. The details of your story—however involved or horrific—are just the tools used to uncover the broader shortcomings. This knowledge is what we need in order to ask God to remove those shortcomings in Steps 6 and 7.

The Conditional Promises of the 5th Step

The 5th Step is followed by some wonderful promises. Most important among them is the beginning of a spiritual experience and some relief from our drink obsession (BB 75:2). These promises are real, but they will quickly disappear if we do not complete all 12 Steps.

REVIEWING THE WORK OF STEPS 1–5

"Returning home we find a place where we can be quiet for an hour, carefully reviewing what we have done. We thank God from the bottom of our heart that we know Him better. Taking this book down from our shelf we turn to the page which contains the twelve steps. Carefully reading the first five proposals we ask if we have omitted anything, for we are building an arch through which we shall walk a free man at last. Is our work solid so far? Are the stones properly in place? Have we skimped on the cement put into the foundation? Have we tried to make mortar without sand?" (BB 75:3).

NOTES ON THE REVIEW

Nowhere else in the Big Book are we asked to stop and review our progress through the steps—considering whether we have taken them to the best of our ability and omitted nothing (BB 75:3). The reason for caution at this stage is clear.

In Steps 6 and 7 we will be seeking God's power to remove those things that block us from him. If we do not fully understand the blockers we identified in the first five steps, we cannot complete Steps 6 and 7 effectively. So we need to be very sure of our work.

We suggest that you take the Big Book down from the shelf, as instructed, and review the first five steps, starting on page 59. In addition, one of the most useful functions of this small book is to provide an outline of the steps and how to take them. Use it to review, as well.

This hour-long review should reveal whether we have "thoroughly followed our path" or not (BB 58:1). It's not a part of any specific step. Many mistakenly believe that this paragraph in the Big Book, particularly its suggested one-hour duration, refers to Steps 6 and 7. That is not the case: "If we can answer to our satisfaction, we then look at Step Six" (BB 76:1). Rather it is an interim review to determine whether we are prepared to proceed with the remaining steps.

Step 6

LETTING GO

"Were entirely ready to have God remove all these defects of character."

Learn about the step: BB 76
Take the step: BB 76:1

"If we can answer to our satisfaction, we then look at step six. We have emphasized willingness as being indispensable. Are we now ready to let God remove from us all the things that we have admitted are objectionable? Can He now take them all—every one? If we still cling to something we will not let go, we ask God to help us be willing." BB 76:1

NOTES ON STEP 6
Willingness to Change

In Step 4 you began to implement your Step 3 decision to move out of your problem of "no power" and into the solution of "power greater than self." To do so, you made an inventory of those manifestations of self that block you from God's healing power.

When this process is complete, you will have "swallowed and digested some big chunks of truth about yourself" (BB 71:0) and become convinced that God can remove whatever self-will blocks you from him.

When you share the nature of your wrongs with God, yourself, and another human in Step 5, you are given conditional promises about the beginning of a spiritual experience and the disappearance of the drinking problem—contingent upon the completion of the twelve-step path (BB 75:2).

You are ready to have God work dramatic change in your life, if you are willing to let go of your old, addiction-driven ways of thinking and acting. Remember, "[s]ome of us have tried to hold on to our old ideas and the result was nil until we let go absolutely" (BB 58:3).

Taking Step 6

This is the direction you receive from Step 6: Let go of your defects of character so God can remove them. If you are not ready to release some of your shortcomings, pray for willingness until it comes.

Self-Will Like a Clenched Fist

The addictive life is like a very tightly clenched fist. It hangs on to old ideas and clutches character defects directed by self-will. We use the fist—with nails digging into our palms—in a futile fight against our addiction and the havoc it causes. We always lose because we have no power over alcohol (BB 45:1).

Our path to recovery is simply opening that fist—letting go. But even with an open hand, we cannot shake free from the defects we once gripped so tightly. We need God to remove them from us.

If you open yourself to God's grace, you are ready for Step 7.

Step 7

LETTING GOD

"Humbly asked Him to remove our shortcomings."

Learn about the step: BB 76
Take the step: BB 76:2

"When ready, we say something like this: 'My Creator, I am now willing that you should have all of me, good and bad. I pray that you now remove from me every single defect of character which stands in the way of my usefulness to you and my fellows. Grant me strength, as I go out from here, to do your bidding. Amen.' We have then completed Step Seven." BB 76:2

NOTES ON STEP 7
Praying for Change

In Step 7 we humbly ask God to change us. The fundamental result of the 12 Steps is a "personality change sufficient to bring about recovery from alcoholism" (BB 567:1; AP 569:1).

We have become willing to change. Now we humbly ask God to do what we cannot do alone (BB 25:2): Remove that which blocks us from usefulness to Him and our fellows (BB 76:2). Remember, this is not a self-help program.

Step 7 is that prayer. The Big Book suggests one to use. So use it. Do not rely simply upon the language of the step. Bill W said we must "turn in all things to the Father of Light who presides over us all" (BB 14:1).

Awareness of Moral Choices

How does God pull this off? Perhaps by simply making us aware of our moral choices. The first six steps are a process of awakening. Awakening to our problem (lack of power), the solution (power greater than self), and the self-will-inspired defects and shortcomings that block us from our God.

When we were drinking, we made whatever choice allowed us to keep drinking. As Bill W put it, "Alcohol was my master" (BB 8:1). With awareness of our character defects, we begin to see the moral choices available to us—we see reality.

These choices involve whether to do things our old way (indulging in self-will and character defects) or to follow God's will (practicing the principles of AA) (BB 25:3; 44:2).

The Proper Use of Our Will

The proper use of our will is to use it when it is lined up with God's will (BB 85:1). And God makes that possible for those who humbly ask.

God will not "zap" you and, for example, free you from dishonesty. That would eliminate our free will. Free will means we always have choices, but alcoholism clouds our view. So we veer away from God's will. Step 7 allows us to become "painfully aware" of our choices: my way or God's way.

"We Claim Spiritual Progress Rather than Spiritual Perfection"

In Step 7, as in the other spiritual steps, we need not and cannot be perfect. But we can show continual progress in our recovery—progress, not perfection, is our goal.

Step 8

PREPARING TO ACT

"Made a list of all persons we had harmed, and became willing to make amends to them all."

Learn about the step: BB 76
Take the step: BB 76:3

WHEN?

"Now we need more action, without which we find that 'Faith without works is dead.'" BB 76:3

How Do We Prepare Our List?

"We have listed the people we have hurt by our conduct, and are willing to straighten out the past if we can." BB 70:3

"We have a list of all persons we have harmed and to whom we are willing to make amends. We made it when we took inventory. We subjected ourselves to a drastic self-appraisal. Now we go out to our fellows and repair the damage done in the past." BB 76:3

How Do We Become Willing?

"We attempt to sweep away the debris which has accumulated out of our effort to live on self-will and run the show ourselves. If we haven't the will to do this, we ask until it comes. Remember it was agreed at the beginning *we would go to any lengths for victory over alcohol.*" BB 76:3

Notes on Step 8

Spirituality, Amends, and Recovery

The amends process is spirituality with legs. You likely carry guilt, shame, and remorse for the harm you caused others. Essentially, you are playing God by condemning yourself. Those feelings block you from God. By becoming willing to make amends for those wrongs, we clear our vision to see God's will in our lives.

Do Not Delay!

The first word in the paragraph that discusses Step 8 is "Now." It guides us both in timing and sequence (BB 76:3).

After completing Steps 6 and 7, we have changed sufficiently to be able to make effective and meaningful amends. We simply did not possess this ability at an earlier stage in our recovery. So "Now" means after Step 7.

"Now" also means that we must not delay in taking this step. Many alcoholics stall out while facing the process of making amends (Steps 8 and 9). And, consequently, they fail to achieve a spiritual awakening and recovery. This is a fatal mistake. "[N]othing worth while can be accomplished" until we undertake Steps 8 and 9 (BB 77:2).

Don't Fall into the Self-Help Trap

You cannot become willing to make amends in the face of your fear, resentment, and hate. You must seek God's solution to your problem by praying for willingness. Again, this is not a self-help program.

Don't Do It Alone!

In both Steps 8 and 9, the help and guidance of your sponsor or spiritual adviser is essential. Why? He or she will keep you moving through the steps at a point that many people falter, help you evaluate whether or not a wrong was actually committed, and offer guidance in determining whether an amends should not or cannot be made. If you take these steps alone, you risk being too hard or too easy on yourself.

Harm to Others Is a Broad Concept

In the Big Book, inventory of harms to others puts much emphasis (perhaps too much) on sexual misconduct (BB 69–71). On the other hand, the Big Book discussion on amends is much broader, covering criminal, financial, personal, and sexual harms, with particular focus on the family. We do not know why Step 4 places such emphasis on sexual harms, but we do know that a proper inventory (and the subsequent amends) should be much more comprehensive. The Big Book discussion concluding Step 4 says as much:

> If we have been thorough about our personal inventory, we have written down a lot. We have listed and analyzed our resentments. We have begun to comprehend their futility and their fatality. We have commenced to see their terrible destructiveness. We have begun to learn tolerance, patience and good will toward all men, even our enemies, for we look on them as sick people. **We have listed the people we have hurt by our conduct**, and are willing to straighten out the past if we can. BB 70:3

Stages of Willingness

Becoming willing is the second action in this step. Willingness may come in stages. We have agreed to go to any length for victory over alcohol (BB 76:3) and to achieve a spiritual experience (BB 79:1). If we lack willingness to make any amend, we are to pray for willingness until it comes (BB 76:3).

Remember, we do not consider the faults of the "other" (BB 78:0). We are in the process of cleaning up our side of the street (BB 77:2).

Making Your List

You have a list of people you have harmed from your 4th Step inventory (BB 76:3). You may want to reconsider the list to be certain that no one was left out or needlessly included.

Make sure you are listing people you actually harmed and you are not seeking forgiveness for a moment of embarrassment that caused no real harm. Remember that the harm you caused may have been a consequence of your drinking—or not. And you may have been sober or not when the harm occurred. A good Step 8 test is to ask if the harm had happened to you, would you expect an amends? And a good example of a circumstance where no amends is appropriate is 12th Step work—no one should need to make amends to someone doing program service to a person in need.

Then group the people on your list into the categories below, according to your willingness to make amends and your practical ability to do so.

Category 1: "Willing Now"

You are ready, willing, and able to make amends immediately to these people.

Include people who are deceased.

Category 2: "Willing Sooner or Later"

You are ready, willing, and able to make amends immediately to these people, but cannot or should not at this time.

Include:

- people who are presently unavailable but will become so
- people whose identity or whereabouts are unknown (but you may eventually identify or find them)
- people who have wounds that are too fresh right now to make meaningful amends to them

Category 3: "Not Willing"

You are not yet ready nor willing to make amends to these people.

Include:

- people you think harmed you more than you harmed them
- people for whom you harbor unresolved resentment or fear
- people you hate
- amends that will cause you big trouble (financial, legal, personal)

After you work through your "Willing Now" and "Willing Sooner or Later" categories of amends, you will probably see the "Not Willing" category in a new light. Perhaps the people in this category will be promoted to one of the others, so you can act.

No Amends to Yourself

Nothing in the Big Book suggests putting yourself on the amends list. After all, in a very short time:

1. the 9th Step promises will start coming true (BB 83:4),
2. you will experience a spiritual awakening (BB 84:2), and
3. your problem will be removed (BB 85:0).

Those gifts will transcend any self-indulgent act that you could fashion for yourself.

Step 9

TAKING ACTION

Made direct amends to such people wherever possible, except when to do so would injure them or others.

Learn about the step: BB 76-84
Take the step: BB 77:0

OUR REAL PURPOSE

"At the moment we are trying to put our lives in order. But this is not an end in itself. Our real purpose is to fit ourselves to be of maximum service to God and the people about us." BB 77:0

GENERAL PRINCIPLES ON AMENDS

"The spiritual life is not a theory. *We have to live it.*" BB 83:2.

"Although these reparations take innumerable forms, there are some general principles which we find guiding. Reminding ourselves that we have decided to go to any lengths to find a spiritual experience, we ask that we be given strength and direction to do the right thing, no matter what the personal consequences may be." BB 79:1

"Before taking drastic action which might implicate other people we secure their consent. If we have obtained permission, have consulted with others, asked God to help and the drastic step is indicated we must not shrink." BB 80:1

"Sometimes we hear an alcoholic say that the only thing he needs to do is to keep sober. Certainly he must keep sober, for there will be no home if he doesn't. But he is yet a long way from making good to the wife or parents whom for years he has so shockingly treated." BB 82:2

"We feel a man is unthinking when he says that sobriety is enough." BB 82:3

"A remorseful mumbling that we are sorry won't fill the bill at all." BB 83:1

How Do We Make Amends?

"Simply we tell him that we will never get over drinking until we have done our utmost to straighten out the past. We are there to sweep off our side of the street, realizing that nothing worthwhile can be accomplished until we do so, never trying to tell him what he should do. His faults are not discussed. We stick to our own. If our manner is calm, frank, and open, we will be gratified with the result." BB 77:2

Making Amends through Spiritual Change

"So we clean house with the family, asking each morning in meditation that our Creator show us the way of patience, tolerance, kindliness and love." BB 83:1

Notes on Step 9

Proper Exceptions to Our Amends List

It is important to remember that almost all amends can be made. That means exceptions to your amends list should be few and limited to the following:

- All persons to whom it is impossible to make amends because you definitely feel they will not meet with you. Discuss what makes you feel that way with your sponsor or spiritual adviser.

- All persons to whom it is impossible to make amends because they are dead, their whereabouts are unknown, or they are otherwise unavailable to you.
- All persons whom you think would be hurt if you tried to make amends. Discuss how you think the person would be hurt with your sponsor or spiritual adviser. Keep in mind that the person hurt by the amends need not be the person to whom the amends is being made.

What an Amend Is Not

Staying sober alone is not making amends, although any amends would be meaningless in the absence of sobriety. Also, apologizing alone is not making amends, though it certainly can be an element of the process of making amends.

Making Tangible Amends

Most alcoholics have very specific, tangible amends that must be made. The Big Book discusses many such amends and how to make them, including financial grievances (BB:78), criminal offenses (BB:78), wrongs involving others (BB:79), and domestic troubles (BB:80). In making these amends, you should consider this advice and consult with your sponsor or spiritual adviser.

Becoming a Changed Person: The Living Amends

The essence of the Big Book is change. The essence of recovery is change. To make amends is to change. Some people will never understand what you are up to. Some will be supportive, even amazed. That is not important. Step 9 is about completing the process of becoming a changed person.

Once again, it is not enough to stay sober or apologize. Being different is the key. Beyond the tangible amends that must be made, living the "family prayer" ideals of "patience, tolerance, kindliness, and love" is the greatest amends of all.

The 9th Step Promises

The Big Book describes the new way of life that has already begun for those just half way through their amends:

> If we are painstaking about this phase of our development, we will be amazed before we are halfway through. We are going to know a new freedom and a new happiness. We will not regret the past nor wish to shut the door on it. We will comprehend the word serenity and we will know peace. No matter how far down the scale we have gone, we will see how our experience can benefit others. That feeling of uselessness and self-pity will disappear. We will lose interest in selfish things and gain interest in our fellows. Self-seeking will slip away. Our whole attitude and outlook upon life will change. Fear of people and of economic insecurity will leave us. We will intuitively know how to handle situations which used to baffle us. We will suddenly realize that God is doing for us what we could not do for ourselves.
>
> Are these extravagant promises? We think not. They are being fulfilled among us—sometimes quickly, sometimes slowly. They will always materialize if we work for them. BB 83:4-84:1

Breaking Down the First Sentence of "The Promises"

If we are painstaking [act with diligence, care, and effort] about this phase of our development [the 9th Step], we will be amazed before we are halfway through [with the amends process]. BB 83:4

The Promises Are:

- The result of working the spiritual program of recovery—taking Steps 3 through 9.
- Evidence of your spiritual awakening—you have entered the world of the Spirit (BB 84:2).
- A description of the (12 Step) principled person you are becoming and the manageable life you are living by working the steps.

Step 10

THE RESULT OF MOVING FROM THE PROBLEM TO THE SOLUTION

"Continued to take personal inventory and when we were wrong promptly admitted it."

Learn about the step: BB 84–85
Take the step: BB 84:2

ENTERING THE "WORLD OF THE SPIRIT"

"This thought brings us to Step Ten, which suggests we continue to take personal inventory and continue to set right any new mistakes as we go along. We vigorously commenced this way of living as we cleaned up the past. We have entered the world of the Spirit. Our next function is to grow in understanding and effectiveness. This is not an overnight matter. It should continue for our lifetime. Continue to watch for selfishness, dishonesty, resentment, and fear. When these crop up, we ask God at once to remove them. We discuss them with someone immediately and make amends quickly if we have harmed anyone. Then we resolutely turn our thoughts to someone we can help. Love and tolerance of others is our code." BB 84:2

REMOVAL OF THE PROBLEM

"And we have ceased fighting anything or anyone—even alcohol. For by this time sanity will have returned. We will seldom be interested in liquor. If tempted, we recoil from it as from a hot flame. We react sanely and normally, and we will find that this has happened automatically. We will see that our new attitude toward liquor has been given us without any thought or effort on our part. It just comes! That is the miracle of it. We are not fighting it, neither are we avoiding temptation. We feel as though we had been placed in a position of neutrality—safe and protected. We have not even sworn off. Instead, the problem has been removed. It does not exist for us. We are neither cocky nor are we afraid. That is our experience. That is how we react so long as we keep in fit spiritual condition" BB 84:3.

MAINTAINING A FIT SPIRITUAL CONDITION

"It is easy to let up on the spiritual program of action and rest on our laurels. We are headed for trouble if we do, for alcohol is a subtle foe. We are not cured of alcoholism. What we really have is a daily reprieve contingent on the maintenance of our spiritual condition. Every day is a day when we must carry the vision of God's will into all of our activities. 'How can I best serve Thee—Thy will (not mine) be done.' These are thoughts which must go with us constantly. We can exercise our will power along this line all we wish. It is the proper use of the will" BB 85:1.

NOTES ON STEP 10

When Do I Take Step 10?

- Timing: "We vigorously commenced this way of living as we cleaned up the past [i.e., while we made amends in Step 9]" (BB 84:2).

- Duration: "This is not an overnight matter. It should continue for our lifetime" (BB 84:2).

How Do I Take Step 10?

Step 10 guides us through the Program of Action every day.

> Continue to watch for selfishness, dishonesty, resentment, and fear [Step 4]. When these crop up, we ask God at once to remove them [Steps 6 and 7]. We discuss them with someone immediately [Step 5] and make amends quickly if we have harmed anyone [Steps 8 and 9]. Then we resolutely turn our thoughts to someone we can help [Step 12]. Love and tolerance of others is our code. BB 84:2

What Is the Result of Taking Steps 1 through 9?

We achieve a spiritual awakening by thoroughly following the path from Steps 1 through 9. The first paragraph of Step 10 makes that abundantly clear:

> We have entered the world of the Spirit. BB 84:2

What Is the Result of Achieving a Spiritual Awakening?

A spiritual awakening brings about the removal of the problem—our obsession—without any thought or action on our part, including "quitting." "We have not even sworn off. Instead, the problem has been removed. It does not exist for us" (BB 85:0).

Our spiritual awakening returns us to sanity regarding our drug of "no choice."

> And we have ceased fighting anything or anyone— even alcohol. For by this time sanity will have returned. BB 84:3

Quite simply, a spiritual awakening or experience is "a personality change sufficient to bring about recovery from alcoholism" (BB 567:1; AP 569:1).

Who Removes the Problem?
God (BB 28:2; 57:0; 120:3).

What Is Our Continuing Responsibility?
"[G]row in understanding and effectiveness" (BB 84:2).

Maintain "a fit spiritual condition" (BB 85:0; 85:1; 100:4).

Caution! "We are not cured of alcoholism. What we really have is a daily reprieve contingent on the maintenance of our spiritual condition" (BB 85:1).

The Best Example of a "Wall Step"
The words of the steps that we see on the walls of meeting rooms are a skeleton of the Program of Action. Those words alone cannot bring you to recovery, though they may offer some relief and comfort. You must read the Big Book and follow its instructions in order to recover.

Step 10 is the best example of how the simple words in a step can prevent you from seeing the full recovery path and process. The word "inventory" in Step 10 refers to the entire Step 4 through 7 process, not just writing a 4th Step inventory—it's the whole spiritual change process practiced on a daily basis. The Big Book explanation of Step 10 makes that eloquently clear (BB 84:2).

Not only do the steps themselves lack the detailed instructions you need to achieve recovery, they also lack a description of the recovered life that can be attained. Many positive and motivating "results" of taking the steps are discussed in the text of the Big Book, including a spiritual awakening and removal of the drinking problem.

So use the language of the steps as a reminder of the underlying principles in the textbook of recovery—the Big Book. Understanding those principles and putting them into action is the key to your recovery.

Step 10 Is a Daily Process

The Big Book gives us nearly identical instructions for Step 10 and the daily, evening review in Step 11—which is coming up next. Consequently, our inventory process should be a daily event, not something to be put off, to be covered in an annual or periodic 4th and 5th Step. Once complete, those steps need not be revisited except as part of the Step 10 and 11 daily inventory. There is no good reason to carry the burden of the day's wrongs from one day into the next—so use the 10th and 11th Step process every day.

Step 11

ENRICHING THE SPIRITUAL EXPERIENCE

"Sought through prayer and meditation to improve our conscious contact with God *as we understood Him*, praying only for knowledge of His will for us and the power to carry that out."

Learn about the step: BB 85–88
Take the step: BB 86–87

"On Awakening . . ."

"On awakening let us think about the twenty-four hours ahead. We consider our plans for the day. Before we begin, we ask God to direct our thinking, especially asking that it be divorced from self-pity, dishonest or self-seeking motives. Under these conditions we can employ our mental faculties with assurance, for after all God gave us brains to use. Our thought-life will be placed on a much higher plane when our thinking is cleared of wrong motives." BB 86:2

"In Thinking About Our Day . . ."

"In thinking about our day we may face indecision. We may not be able to determine which course to take. Here we ask God for inspiration, an intuitive thought or a decision. We relax and take it easy. We don't struggle. We are often surprised how the right answers come after we have tried this for a while. What used to be the hunch or the occasional inspiration gradually becomes a working part of the mind. Being still inexperienced and having just made conscious contact with God, it is not probable that we are going to be inspired at all times. We might pay for this presumption in all sorts of absurd actions and ideas. Nevertheless, we find that our thinking will, as time passes, be more and more on the plane of inspiration. We come to rely upon it." BB 86:3

"As We Go Through the Day . . ."

"As we go through the day we pause, when agitated or doubtful, and ask for the right thought or action. We constantly remind ourselves we are no longer running the show, humbly saying to ourselves many times each day 'Thy will be done.'" BB 87:3

"When We Retire at Night . . ."

"When we retire at night, we constructively review our day. Were we resentful, selfish, dishonest or afraid? Do we owe an apology? Have we kept something to ourselves which should be discussed with another person at once? Were we kind and loving toward all? What could we have done better? Were we thinking of ourselves most of the time? Or were we thinking of what we could do for others, of what we could pack into the stream of life? But we must be careful not to drift into worry, remorse or morbid reflection, for that would diminish our usefulness to others. After making our review we ask God's forgiveness and inquire what corrective measures should be taken." BB 86:1

NOTES ON STEP 11

The Result of a Prayerful Life

It is easy to refer to Step 11 as the prayer and meditation step. After all, the Big Book itself describes it that way ("Step Eleven suggests prayer and meditation." BB 85:3). But prayer and meditation are merely the tools we use to achieve the true purpose of Step 11—improved intimacy with the God of our understanding.

We use these tools to "grow in [spiritual] understanding and effectiveness" (BB 84:2) and to maintain a fit spiritual condition (BB 85:0; 85:1; 100:4). We do not pray to have God bless our plan. We pray to have God reveal his plan to us and for the power to carry it out.

As we become more aware of God's plan in our lives— more awake—making the choice between self-will and God's will becomes easier. Most of the time we will intuitively know what God would have us do. When we are asked to choose between two seemingly right paths, prayer is an especially powerful spiritual tool.

We do not pray for "our own selfish ends" (BB 87:1), as "[m]any of us have wasted a lot of time doing that and it doesn't work" (BB 87:1). It is just a further example of our self-centeredness—our need to control (BB 60–62). We ultimately must come to understand that God's plan is far superior to our own. ("[W]e realize that the things which came to us when we put ourselves in God's hands were better than anything we could have planned." BB 100:1)

When we maintain constant contact with God in this way:

We are then in much less danger of excitement, fear, anger, worry, self-pity, or foolish decisions.

We become much more efficient. We do not tire so easily, for we are not burning up energy foolishly as we did when we were trying to arrange life to suit ourselves. It works—it really does. BB 88:0; 88:1

Prayer Instructions in the Big Book

This chart identifies the specific Big Book instructions for prayer. You may choose to incorporate some of these prayers into your daily practices, as do the morning and evening prayers (*see* appendix B).

Name	Chapter	Page	Paragraph
Bill's Prayer	Bill's Story (1)	13	4
Step 3 Prayer	How It Works (5)	63	2
Resentment Prayer	How It Works (5)	67	0
Fear Prayer	How It Works (5)	68	3
Sex Prayer I	How It Works (5)	69	2
Sex Prayer II	How It Works (5)	69	3
Sex Prayer III	How It Works (5)	70	2
Step 5 Prayer	Into Action (6)	75	3
Step 6 Prayer	Into Action (6)	76	1
Step 7 Prayer	Into Action (6)	76	2
Step 8 Prayer	Into Action (6)	76	3
Amends Prayer I	Into Action (6)	79	1
Amends Prayer II	Into Action (6)	80	1
Jealousy Prayer	Into Action (6)	82	1
Family Prayer	Into Action (6)	83	1
Step 10 Prayer	Into Action (6)	84	2
"God's Will" Prayer	Into Action (6)	85	1
Step 11 Evening Prayer	Into Action (6)	86	1
Step 11 Morning Prayer I	Into Action (6)	86	2
Step 11 Morning Prayer II	Into Action (6)	87	1
Step 11 Daily Prayer	Into Action (6)	87	3
Step 12 Prayer	A Vision For You (11)	164	2

Two Prayers Based on Big Book Directions

For some of us, prayer is difficult. We simply don't know how to begin. The Big Book tells us that we can seek the guidance of our religious and spiritual advisers:

> Be quick to see where religious people are right.
> Make use of what they offer. BB 87:2

It also recommends that we "select and memorize a few set prayers which emphasize the principles we have been discussing" (BB 87:2).

In appendix B of this book are two suggested prayers—one for the morning and one for the evening—that are based entirely upon the directions in the Big Book. The Big Book page and paragraph references are included throughout the prayers.

Remember always, the central focus of your prayers should be: "How can I best serve Thee—Thy will (not mine) be done" (BB 85:1).

Remain to Pray

"I earnestly advise every alcoholic to read this book through, and though perhaps he came to scoff, he may remain to pray." —William D. Silkworth, M.D., *The Doctor's Opinion* (BB: xxxii:2; AP xxx:2).

Step 12

LEADING A RECOVERED LIFE

"Having had a spiritual awakening as the result of these steps, we tried to carry this message to alcoholics, and to practice these principles in all our affairs."

Learn about the step: BB 59-60, 89-103; 569-70
Take the step: BB 89:1 (carry message) &
59-60 (practice principles)

CARRY THE MESSAGE TO ALCOHOLICS

"It is a most wonderful blessing to be relieved of the terrible curse with which I was afflicted. My health is good and I have regained my self-respect and the respect of my colleagues. My home life is ideal and my business is as good as can be expected in these uncertain times. I spend a great deal of time passing on what I learned to others who want and need it badly. I do it for four reasons:

Sense of duty.

It is a pleasure.

Because in so doing I am paying my debt to the man who took time to pass it on to me.

Because every time I do it I take out a little more insurance for myself against a possible slip." "Dr. Bob's Nightmare," BB 180:3

WHAT SHOULD A RECOVERED PERSON LOOK FOR IN A PROSPECT?

That he wants to recover or quit: "If he does not want to stop drinking, don't waste time trying to persuade him." BB 90:1

That he is coming off a binge: "Wait for the end of the spree, or at least for a lucid interval." BB 90:3

That he is not drunk: "Don't deal with him when he is very drunk." BB 90:3

That he wants to go to any extreme to stop: "Then let his family or a friend ask him if he wants to quit for good and if he would go to any extreme to do so. If he says yes, then his attention should be drawn to you as a person who has recovered." BB 90:3

That he is depressed: "He may be more receptive when depressed." BB 91:2

That he is hopeless: "The more hopeless he feels, the better." BB 94:1

WHAT SHOULD A RECOVERED PERSON CONVEY TO A PROSPECT?

That he is "one of a fellowship who, as part of their own recovery, try to help others and who will be glad to talk to him if he cares to see you." BB 90:3

His own drinking history. BB 91:3

That he is an alcoholic. BB 91:4

The hopelessness of the problem of mind and body. BB 92:1, 92:2

The reality of the mental obsession. BB 92:1

That alcoholism is an illness—a fatal malady. BB 92:2

The spiritual solution as experienced by the recovered person. BB 93:0

That to recover the prospect must be willing to believe in a power greater than himself and live by spiritual principles. BB 93:0

That unselfish, constructive action is necessary. BB 93:2

An outline of the "12 Step Program of Action." BB 94:1

That the prospect owes him nothing because passing on the program is a vital part of his recovery. BB 94:1

The need to place the welfare of others above self. BB 94:1

A description of the Fellowship of Alcoholics Anonymous. BB 94:2

An offer of friendship and fellowship. BB 95:1

A Big Book. BB 94:2

A relationship with God is essential and dependence upon Him must come first. BB 98:2, 100:0, 100:1

"Burn the idea into the consciousness of every man that he can get well regardless of anyone. The only condition is that he trust in God and clean house." BB 98:2

PRACTICING THESE PRINCIPLES IN ALL OUR AFFAIRS

"Rarely have we seen a person fail who has thoroughly followed our path." BB 58:1

"Do not be discouraged. No one among us has been able to maintain anything like perfect adherence to these principles." BB 60:1

"We have entered the world of the Spirit. Our next function is to grow in understanding and effectiveness." BB 84:2

"What we really have is a daily reprieve contingent on the maintenance of our spiritual condition. Every day is a day when we must carry the vision of God's will into all of our activities. 'How can I best serve Thee—Thy will (not mine) be done.'" BB 85:1

"Follow the dictates of a Higher Power and you will presently live in a new and wonderful world, no matter what your present circumstances!" BB 100:1

"Assuming we are spiritually fit, we can do all sorts of things alcoholics are not supposed to do." BB 100:4

"Abandon yourself to God as you understand God. Admit your faults to Him and to your fellows. Clear away the wreckage of your past. Give freely of what you find and join us. We shall be with you in the Fellowship of the Spirit, and you will surely meet some of us as you trudge the Road of Happy Destiny." BB 164:3

THROUGH THE RECOVERY ARCH TO A CHANGED LIFE

The spiritual experience or awakening is a "personality change sufficient to bring about recovery from alcoholism." BB 567:1 (AP 569:1)

"The great fact is just this, and nothing less: That we have had deep and effective spiritual experiences which have revolutionized our whole attitude toward life, toward our fellows and toward God's universe. The central fact of our lives today is the absolute certainty that our Creator has entered into our hearts and lives in a way which is indeed miraculous. He has commenced to accomplish those things for us which we could never do by ourselves." BB 25:2

NOTES ON STEP 12

Carrying the Message Is Essential to a Recovered Life

Bill W and Dr. Bob—and the first hundred that followed— knew from the start that helping others was essential to their own continued recovery. Carrying the message is not simple altruism, but is essential to our spiritual fitness and, thus, our continued sobriety. Throughout the Big Book this theme is repeated over and over: "Practical experience shows that nothing will so much insure immunity from drinking as intensive work with other alcoholics" (BB 89:1). Bill W first learned this principle from his friend Ebby Thatcher, as recounted in "Bill's Story," here:

> My friend had emphasized the absolute necessity of demonstrating these principles in all my affairs. Particularly was it imperative to work with others as he had worked with me. 'Faith without works was dead,' he said. And how appallingly true for the alcoholic! For if an alcoholic failed to perfect and enlarge his spiritual life through work and self-sacrifice for others, he could not survive the certain trials and low spots ahead. If he did not work, he would surely drink again, and if he drank, he would surely die. Then faith would be dead indeed. With us it is just like that. BB 14:6

The Fallacy of Relapse Prevention Rules

Some individuals counsel recovered people against associating with particular persons, places, and things that may "trigger" a return to drinking. This thinking is directly contrary to the teaching of the Big Book (BB 100–103). As long as we maintain our spiritual fitness and act with proper motives, "we can do all sorts of things alcoholics are not supposed to do" (BB 100:4) and "visit the most sordid spot on earth" to be of help to others (BB 102:2). Of course, this principle does not apply to those who have not completed the Program of Action and achieved recovery.

When Does the Spiritual Awakening Occur?

The first phrase of Step 12 can be confusing. The language—"[h]aving had a spiritual awakening as the result of these steps"—is descriptive of the message that we must carry, not when the awakening occurs in the step process. Our spiritual awakening and the resulting personality change have already occurred as we progress through Steps 9 and 10 and "[w]e have entered the world of the Spirit" (BB 84:2).

What Does It Mean to Practice These Principles in "All Our Affairs?"

The principles are the "design for living" that the Big Book describes: "A new life has been given us or, if you prefer, 'a design for living' that really works" (BB 28:2). They solve all our problems, not simply our obsession with alcohol.

Simple abstinence from alcohol is not recovery. "We feel that elimination of our drinking is but a beginning. A much more important demonstration of our principles lies before us in our respective homes, occupations and affairs" (BB 19:1).

Qualities for a Sponsor

While the Big Book does not specifically discuss sponsorship, today sponsors are the mainstay of educating newcomers in the twelve-step process. The Big Book does provide guidance for those carrying the message, and the desired qualities for the messenger (or sponsor) are inherent in the text. At a minimum, a sponsor should be a person who:

- Has had a spiritual awakening or experience as the result of his or her journey through the 12 Steps;

- Has had the obsession to drink removed without any thought or effort on their part;
- Has a sponsor of his or her own; and
- Knows and follows Big Book directions.

A sponsor is not a counselor but rather a teacher and a guide. Sponsors should not run the lives of their sponsees nor should they become life coaches. Their role is to pass on the message of their recovery and how others can achieve a similar outcome. This simple method of one person helping another is how AA has grown to benefit millions.

A Final Story:

HUMPTY DUMPTY AND THE HAND OF GOD

O nce upon a time or in the recent present—it changes with the telling—Humpty Dumpty held the Hand of God. Sometimes he gripped it firmly, at other times lightly, barely touching, but the Hand of God was always there, even though God did not grab or clutch at Humpty's hand.

Humpty Dumpty could do many things. He could:

Sit and stand

Walk and run

Skip and leap

and varied other things, none of which he thought too much about. He just did them.

Now others saw this, and they approved of Humpty and considered him an excellent fellow. The King and all the King's men and even all the King's horses thought well of him, and Humpty Dumpty, whenever he chanced to look at himself, was pleased with what he saw in a vague sort of way, and, if he had ever been asked, would have said that he was reasonably contented.

One day, for no particular reason, and without really giving it any thought, Humpty Dumpty did all these things without touching God's Hand. When he realized what he had done, he was amazed that he had been able to

Sit and stand

Walk and run

Skip and leap

and varied other things, all of which made him extremely proud and quite self-satisfied.

So he kept on this way without ever reaching up; and he considered that he was doing very well indeed, though at times he felt an unusual loneliness and was often frightened—for no reason he could see—and, because of a strange uneasy feeling, he kept trying to do more and more.

Now the others—the King, his men, and even his horses— noticed that Humpty was not doing things well at all, and although they said nothing to him about it, it made them wonder and feel sad.

Of course, doing more and more exhausted Humpty, and one day . . .

Humpty Dumpty sat on a wall.

Humpty Dumpty had a great fall.

All the King's horses

And all the King's men

Couldn't put Humpty together again.

Now, as it turned out, only Humpty Dumpty could do that. And the only way sad, shattered Humpty accomplished that was by becoming willing to touch God's Hand again, nothing more: if one can call that "doing." You see, he realized that he was broken and all apart. He saw with bright clarity that neither he himself nor others could mend him.

But he remembered the touch of God's Hand.

Now, we don't know if Humpty did this entirely by himself, or if even in this he received help, but slowly, haltingly, from the pathetic wreckage that was Humpty Dumpty, a poor, battered, broken hand just STARTED to reach up, and suddenly God's Hand was there, and Humpty's hand touched it. Right then, or gradually—it changes with the telling—Humpty Dumpty became whole again, sound and complete. And he could:

Sit and stand

Walk and run

Skip and leap

and varied other things, all of which he did with exquisite awareness and a grateful heart.

Now while the King, his men, and even his horses thought well of him again, what mattered most to Humpty was that he again liked himself and perhaps even, for the first time, loved himself, that he was quietly content, and that, from time to time, he was quite happy.

Humpty Dumpty grasped the Hand of God, as tightly as he could, knowing now, full well, that as long as he did so, he would never fall again.

By Paul Hilton.

Appendix A

STEP 4 WORKSHEETS

Fourth Step Inventory – Resentments: My Grudge List

"On our grudge list we set opposite each name our injuries." (BB 65:1)

I Resent (BB 65:2)	The Cause (BB 65:2)	What part of "self" was injured or threatened? (BB 65:1)							
People, institutions, or principles with whom I am angry (BB 64:3)	Why am I angry? (BB 64:3)	Self-Esteem	Financial Security	Physical Security	Personal Relations	Sex Relations	Ambitions	Pride	

For Each Resentment Pray:

"God, help me show [person, institution, or principle] the same tolerance, pity, and patience that [I] would cheerfully grant a sick friend." (BB 67:0)

89

Fourth Step Inventory – Resentments: My Inventory

"Putting out of our minds the wrongs others had done, we resolutely looked for our own mistakes."
(BB 67:2)

How did my behavior contribute to the situation causing the anger or perpetuating anger into resentment? Be specific. (BB 67:2)	Exact nature of my wrongs?				
	Dishonesty	Selfishness	Fear	Inconsideration	Self-Centeredness or Need to Control

Fourth Step Inventory—Fear

"We reviewed our fears thoroughly. We put them on paper, even though we had no resentment in connection with them. We asked ourselves why we had them."

(BB 68:1)

What am I afraid of?
(BB 68:1)

For Each Fear Pray:
"God, please remove my fear of _____ and direct my attention to what you would have me be." (BB 68:3)

Source of my fears?
How did "self-reliance" fail us?
(BB 68:1)

	Self-Centeredness or Need to Control	Self-Esteem	Physical Security	Financial Security	Personal Relations	Sex Relations	Ambitions	Pride

Fourth Step Inventory — Other Harms

"We have listed the people we have hurt by our conduct. . . ."
(BB 70:3)

Harms Prayer: *"God, please mold my ideals and help me live up to them."* (BB 69:2)

Who have I hurt? (BB 69:1)	What did I do? (BB 69:1)	What motivated my behavior?						Exact nature of my wrongs?						Notes
		Self Esteem	Pride	Personal Relationships	Physical Security	Financial Security	Ambition	Dishonesty	Selfishness	Fear	Inconsideration	Self-Centeredness or Need to Control	Resentment	New ideals: What should I have done, and what are possible amends? (BB 69-70)

Fourth Step Inventory – Sexual Harms

"We reviewed our own conduct over the years past."
(BB 69:1)

Who have I hurt? (BB 69:1)	What did I do? (BB 69:1)	Did I arouse?			What motivated my behavior?						Exact nature of my wrongs?						Notes:
		Jealousy	Suspicion	Bitterness	Self-Esteem	Pride	Personal Relationships	Physical Security	Financial Security	Ambition	Dishonesty	Selfishness	Fear	Inconsideration	Need to Control	Self-Centeredness or	Resentment	New Ideals: What should I have done, and what are possible amends? (BB 69-70)

Sex Prayer: *"To sum up about sex: We earnestly pray for the right ideal, for guidance in each questionable situation, for sanity, and for the strength to do the right thing."* (BB 70:2)

Appendix B

SUGGESTED MORNING AND EVENING PRAYERS

A MORNING PRAYER

God, please direct my thinking. Please let it be free of self-pity. Please free my motives from dishonesty and self-seeking.	BB 86:2 This first paragraph is to be done literally "upon awakening," before you turn off the alarm, before your feet hit the floor. The rest can be done slightly later.
Thank you for this good day. Thank you for the privilege you have given me of being in this day.	We often describe the day as sunny, beautiful, cold, snowy, etc.
In this good day I acknowledge my powerlessness over alcohol—the unmanageability of my life.	BB 30:2, 59:2, and many others.
Please take my will and my life.	BB 59:2, 63:2
Thank you very much for your daily reprieve, your gift of sobriety.	BB 85:1
Please grant me an awareness of, and gratitude for, the goodness and miracle of your gift throughout this day.	BB 85:0
Please let me use your gift in a way that pleases you and helps others.	BB 77:0
Lord, give me thoughts, words, and silence that will be helpful to others.	BB 89:1, 89:3, 102:2
Grant me knowledge of your will for me and the power to carry that out.	BB 59:2, 85:1, 87:3
Creator, please lead me this day in the way of patience, tolerance, kindliness, and love.	BB 83:1
Show me what I can do today to help the person who is still sick.	BB 164:2
Amen.	

AN EVENING PRAYER

Thank you, God, for my daily reprieve—your gift of sobriety.	BB 85:2
Please help me honestly review this day, without worry, remorse, or morbid reflection.	BB 86:1
Was I resentful?	BB 84:2, 86:1
Was I selfish?	BB 84:2, 86:1
Was I dishonest?	BB 84:2, 86:1
Was I afraid?	BB 84:2, 86:1
If I was, please remove these defects from me.	BB 86:1
I commit to discuss them with another person and make amends quickly, if I harmed anyone.	BB 84:2
Was I patient?	BB 67:0, 70:3, 83:1, 86:3, 118:2
Was I kind?	BB 67:1, 83:1, 86:1
Was I tolerant?	BB 67:0, 67:1, 70:3, 83:1, 84:2, 118:2
Was I loving?	BB 83:1, 84:2, 86:1, 118:2
God, please forgive me and grant me knowledge of what changes in my life I should make.	BB 86:1
Help me be of maximum service to you and others.	BB 77:0, 164:2
Lord, today I remember these people in my prayer to you: _____.	BB 84:2 Turn your thoughts to others by remembering them in your prayers.
Amen.	

NOTES

NOTES

NOTES

NOTES

NOTES

NOTES

NOTES

NOTES

NOTES

NOTES

ABOUT THE AUTHORS

*B*oth of the authors owe their recovery from alcoholism and, consequently, their lives to the Big Book, *Alcoholics Anonymous.*

Paul H. searched for a solution to his alcoholism for many years—finding only frustration in the ideas he now understands to be human by nature and destined to fail. In the depths of his alcoholism, he followed some wonderful advice from a dedicated skid row detox attendant to "find himself in the Big Book." He did, and in so doing discovered his real problem: lack of power over alcohol. He also found a solution to that problem: a power greater than himself. The Big Book taught him the "spiritual program of action" he needed to achieve recovery and grow in the solution. As part of that recovery, he began recording his understanding of the principles in the Big Book, so he could pass on those ideas in a simple, direct way to newcomers, sponsors, and others interested in the program. This small book is the culmination of refining those thoughts for many years.

Scott N. spent three months in treatment in half a year's time. The solution to his problem still eluded him until he immersed himself in the Big Book, accepted the help of his sponsor—the co-author of this book—and used the predecessor to this book as his guide through the steps. He finds continued strength in supporting the efforts of his sponsor, including the publication of this book, and passing on what he has learned to those he sponsors.

Years of working together as sponsor-sponsee and group settings have allowed the authors to bring this book to its present, albeit imperfect, form. The process will continue as their understanding, spiritual experience, and recovery progresses. They welcome any suggestions, comments, and criticisms, with the warning that any information shared may become evident in future editions of this book.

While the work of recovery may at times be difficult, the program itself is one of extreme simplicity. The farewell remarks from Dr. Bob, AA's co-founder, are a poignant reminder of that fact. The authors hope that this volume contributes to the elegant simplicity advocated by Dr. Bob.

Dr. Bob's Farewell Remarks

There are two or three things that flashed into my mind on which it would be fitting to lay a little emphasis. One is the simplicity of our program. Let's not louse it all up with Freudian complexes and things that are interesting to the scientific mind, but have very little to do with our actual A.A. work. Our Twelve Steps, when simmered down to the last, resolve themselves into the words "love" and "service." We understand what love is, and we understand what service is. So let's bear those two things in mind.

Let us also remember to guard that erring member— the tongue—and if we must use it, let's use it with kindness and consideration and tolerance.

And one more thing: None of us would be here today if somebody hadn't taken time to explain things to us, to give us a little pat on the back, to take us to a meeting or two, to do numerous little kind and thoughtful acts in our behalf. So let us never get such a degree of smug complacency that we're not willing to extend, or attempt to extend, to our less fortunate brothers that help which has been so beneficial to us.

Sunday, July 30, 1950
First International AA Convention
Cleveland, Ohio

For more information regarding this book, go to **www. SimpleButNotEasy.org.** There you can (1) communicate with the authors, (2) download Fourth Step worksheets, suggested prayers, and other helpful materials, (3) learn where to buy additional copies of *Simple But Not Easy*, and (4) see a calendar of upcoming twelve-step seminars featuring the authors.

CPSIA information can be obtained at www.ICGtesting.com
Printed in the USA
LVOW05s1436211213

366348LV00001B/1/P